W9-CAZ-136

DISCARD

Other Books in the
Science for Kids Series

Science For Kids
39 EASY
PLANT BIOLOGY
EXPERIMENTS

Science For Kids
39 EASY
PLANT BIOLOGY
EXPERIMENTS

Robert W. Wood
Illustrated by John T. Fitzgerald

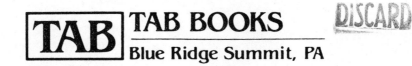

TAB | **TAB BOOKS**
Blue Ridge Summit, PA

FIRST EDITION
FIRST PRINTING

© 1991 by **TAB Books**.
TAB Books is a division of McGraw-Hill, Inc.

Library of Congress Cataloging-in-Publication Data

Wood, Robert W., 1933 –
    Science for kids : 39 easy plant biology experiments / by Robert
W. Wood.
        p.   cm.
    Includes index.
    Summary: Presents thirty-nine experiments with plants, including
''Why Plants Have Roots,'' ''How a Bean Grows,'' and ''How to Graft a
Plant.''
    ISBN 0-8306-1941-0 (h)   ISBN 0-8306-1935-6 (p)
    1. Botany—Experiments—Juvenile literature. 2. Gardening-
-Experiments—Juvenile literature.   [1. Plants—Experiments.
2. Botany—Experiments. 3. Experiments.]   I. Title.
QK52.6.W66   1991
581'.C78—dc20   91-12059
                                              CIP
                                               AC

TAB Books offers software for sale. For information and a catalog, please contact
TAB Software Department, Blue Ridge Summit, PA 17294-0850.

Acquisitions Editor: Kimberly Tabor
Book Editor: Yvonne Yoder
Production: Katherine G. Brown
Book Design: Jaclyn J. Boone   SFK
Cover photo by Susan Riley, Harrisonburg, VA

Contents

Acknowledgments

Illustrations by John T. Fitzgerald
Additional illustrations by John David Wood

Acknowledgments

Illustrations by John T. Fitzgerald
Additional illustrations by John David Wood

Introduction

The Science for Kids series consists of eight books introducing astronomy, chemistry, meteorology, geology, engineering, plant biology, animal biology, and geography.

Science is a subject that instantly becomes exciting with even simple discoveries. On any day, and at any time, we can see these mysteries unfold around us.

The series was written to open the door, and to invite the curious to enter—to explore, to think, and to wonder. To realize that anyone can experiment and learn. To discover that the only thing you really need to study science is a curious mind. The rest of the material is all around you. It is there for anyone to see. You have only to look.

Biology is one of the oldest sciences. It is the study of living things and everything about them. Some of the differences between living things and nonliving things are that living things take in and use food. They grow and produce more of their own kind. Biology is normally divided into two main groups; the study of animals, called *zoology*, and the study of plants, called *botany*. This book is about the study of plants.

In our earth's history, plants influenced our distant ancestors long before our ancestors were able to influence plants. Early man used things as he found them, and moved from one place to another, partly because of the need to search for food. Plants were an important food source. People in mild climates that lived near fresh-water marshes ate rice or similar plants from these wet lands.

The lives of most of the early Indians living east of the upper Mississippi River depended on growing corn. Some tribes in the far west depended more on acorns, while the Bitterroot Indians of the Northwest got their name from the roots of the plant that provided them with most of their food.

Early cave dwellers wore grass sandals and used burning reeds for torches to find their way underground. Plants provided protection from the weather in the form of clothing and shelters. Plants were a source of weapons such as clubs, spears and bows and arrows. They became a way to get around in the form of rafts and boats, and even provided most of the medicines.

Today we still depend on plants for food, shelter and medicines. As vast stores of oil in the earth are used up, plants might be considered more as a source of fuel. Plants are now bred and improved for a variety of purposes. For example, the taste of tomatoes has been improved, and some plants now supply us with more vitamins. Some new types of corn have stronger roots so that the plant can stand in high winds. And other plants have been bred to produce food earlier in the growing season, or for a longer growing period.

Trees are the largest plants of all. They never stop growing while they are alive. They shelter the earth from the sun and the drying winds. Their fallen leaves catch the rain and allow it to soak slowly into the ground. Without trees, rain would fall on dry, hard ground and run off across the fields, washing away topsoil and leaving deep gullies. Trees also provide beauty and shade for our lawns, parks and highways.

We now know that cutting down a lot of trees can actually change our environment. Plants take in carbon dioxide and give off oxygen as a result of photosynthesis. Photosynthesis is a food-making process where green plants combine energy from light with water and carbon dioxide to make food. Animals take in oxygen and give off carbon dioxide when they breathe. If plants were suddenly to stop this chemical activity, most of the oxygen in our atmosphere would disappear.

Oxygen is normally not found on other planets and stars in the same form as on earth. The earth is the only planet in the solar system with an atmosphere that always contains large amounts of free oxygen. This means that no other planet in the solar system has as many living things as our earth.

The oxygen in our atmosphere depends on a fine balance held by the chemical activities of green plants. It seems that our lives depend on how well we preserve our plant life. Anyone with a strong interest in plants, and the proper educational background, will have many opportunities to ensure a healthy environment for our future. These experiments will provide an introduction to the fascinating study of plants.

Symbols Used in this Book

All of the experiments in this book can be done safely, but young children should be instructed to use caution at the stove, and when working with sharp knives. They should be warned of the hazards associated with carelessness. The following symbols are used throughout the book for you to use as a guide to what children might be able to do independently, and what they **should not do** without adult supervision. Keep in mind that some children might not be mature enough to do any of the experiments without adult help, and that these symbols should be used as a guide only and do not replace good judgment of parents or teachers.

 Materials or tools used in this experiment could be dangerous in young hands. Adult supervision is recommended. Children should be instructed on the care and handling of sharp tools and how to protect surfaces.

 Protective gloves that are heat resistant should be worn. Hot objects can burn hands. Protect surfaces beneath hot materials—do not set pots of boiling water directly on tabletops or counters. Use towels or heat pads.

 A stove might be used to boil water in this project and adult supervision is required. Keep other small children away from boiling water and burners.

1

How Plants Prevent Erosion

Materials
- WEED OR UNWANTED PLANT
- WATER

Soften the ground around the plant with water (Fig. 1-1). Then grab the plant around the stem, near the ground, and carefully pull it from the dirt (Fig. 1-2). Examine the roots (Fig. 1-3). You should see the roots still clinging to a small amount of soil (Fig. 1-4).

Running water is the greatest cause of erosion. Roots from plants grow down through the dirt and hold the soil together (Fig. 1-5). This helps prevent the soil from being washed away.

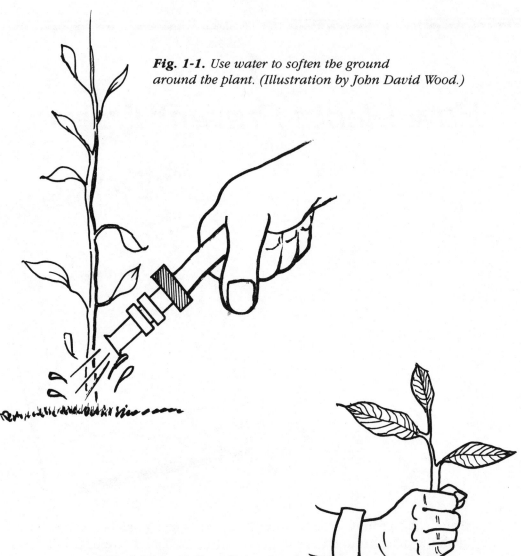

Fig. 1-1. *Use water to soften the ground around the plant. (Illustration by John David Wood.)*

Fig. 1-2. *Carefully pull the plant from the ground.*

Fig. 1-3. *Look closely at the roots. (Illustration by John David Wood.)*

Fig. 1-4. *The roots will be holding a small mass of soil.*

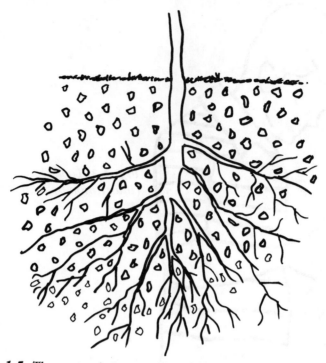

Fig. 1-5. *The roots of plants help hold the soil together to prevent erosion.*

2

Why Plants Have Roots

Materials

- FRESH STALK OF CELERY WITH LEAVES
- LARGE BOWL
- JAR
- KNIFE
- RED FOOD COLORING
- WATER
- TWEEZERS

Fill the jar about half full of water and add a few drops of food coloring (Fig. 2-1). Fill the bowl about half full of water. Now place the lower end of the celery in the bowl and, keeping it under water, cut about an inch from the bottom of the stalk. Now place the stalk in the jar of red water and let it stand until the leaves are colored red (Fig. 2-2).

Examine the celery and notice the red color in the stalk and the leaves. Cut across the stem and you will see the tubes that carry the water (Fig. 2-3). You can even separate the stem with tweezers and follow the red streaks up to the leaves. This is the path the water takes when the plant is growing in the ground.

The roots take in water and dissolved minerals, not through the part of the root that has a tough, thick covering, but through the tiny white thread-like parts called root hairs. Water and dissolved minerals pass through the thin walls of the root hairs, up through the roots, then through the tubes to the leaves. This is how plants get their food.

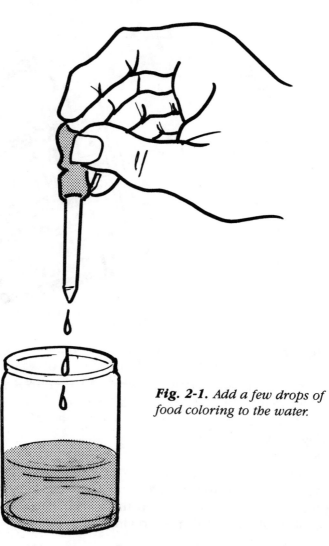

Fig. 2-1. Add a few drops of food coloring to the water.

Fig. 2-2. Place the stalk in the colored water and let it stand.

Fig. 2-3. Tubes carry the water through the stalk to the leaves. (Illustration by John David Wood.)

3
Why Plants Have Leaves

Materials
- POTTED PLANT
- THIN CARDBOARD OR PAPER
- PAPER CLIP
- SCISSORS

Cut two pieces of cardboard the same size. Each side should be 1 inch long (Fig. 3-1). Place one piece on top and one on the bottom of a leaf near the top of the plant (Fig. 3-2). Fasten the pieces in place with the paper clip (Fig. 3-3). Next, place the plant in a sunny location for a few days (Fig. 3-4). Now remove the paper clip and the pieces of cardboard. Examine the leaf and notice the area that did not get sunlight.

You should see that this area is a lighter color (Fig. 3-5). This is because the plant was unable to produce *chlorophyll* in the area covered by the pieces of cardboard. The word chlorophyll comes from two Greek words, meaning light-green leaf. Chlorophyll is in the form of tiny green specks grouped against the inside walls of the cells in the leaf. They give the leaf its green color.

Green plants must have carbon dioxide, water, minerals, and chlorophyll to make food. To do this, they must have light. The green leaves change light energy into chemical energy and the chemical energy is used to make food. This process is called *photosynthesis*. Photo means light and synthesis means putting together. So the term means putting together by light.

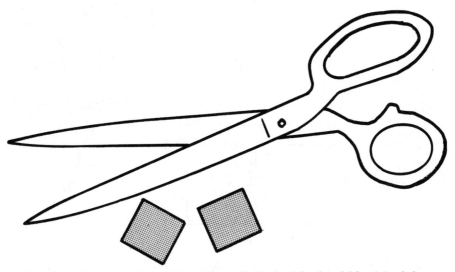

Fig. 3-1. *Cut two pieces of cardboard. Each side should be 1 inch long.*

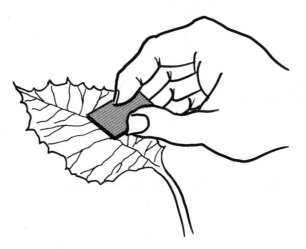

Fig. 3-2. *Place one on top and one on the bottom of a leaf.*

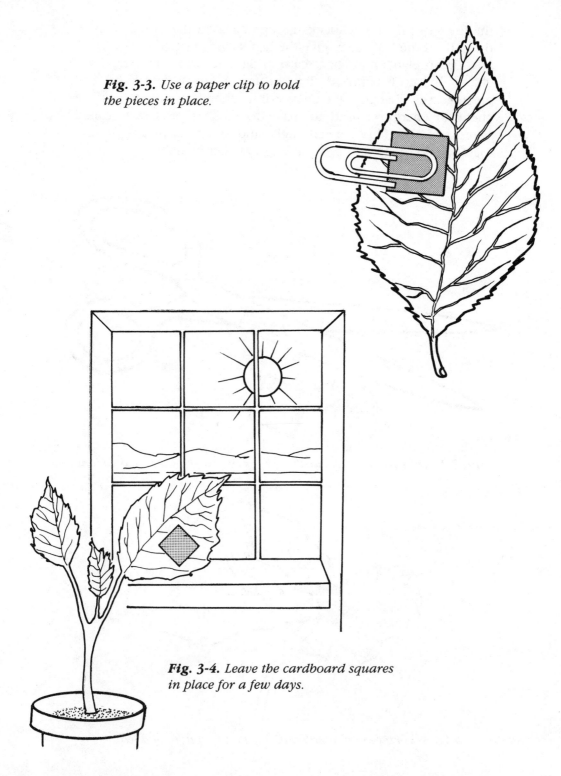

Fig. 3-3. Use a paper clip to hold the pieces in place.

Fig. 3-4. Leave the cardboard squares in place for a few days.

Fig. 3-5. *The area under the cardboard is a lighter color.*

4

How Plants Breathe

Materials
- GROWING PLANT WITH LEAVES
- PETROLEUM JELLY

Apply a thin coat of petroleum jelly to the bottom surface of one of the leaves (Fig. 4-1). Next, apply a thin coat to the top surface of a nearby leaf (Fig. 4-2). Leave the coatings in place for a day or two. Now examine both leaves (Fig. 4-3). You will see that the leaf with the petroleum jelly on the bottom surface will be dying.

Tiny air holes, called *stomata*, so small they can only be seen through a microscope, are on the underside of the leaf. Stomata means little mouths. These holes are valves that open and close to bring in air and to give off water (Fig. 4-4). One of these valves is called a stoma. They usually open in daylight and close in darkness. There are many thousands to a square inch of leaf surface. The petroleum jelly sealed the holes so that the leaf couldn't breathe and started to die. Some leaves, however, have their stomata in their upper surfaces. The water lily, for example, must have its air holes in the upper surface because the lower surface is always in water.

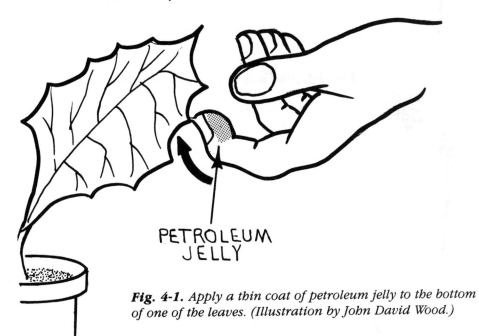

PETROLEUM
JELLY

Fig. 4-1. Apply a thin coat of petroleum jelly to the bottom of one of the leaves. (Illustration by John David Wood.)

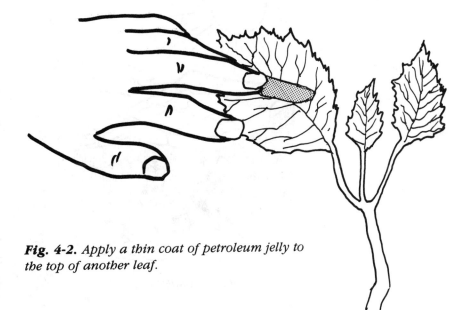

Fig. 4-2. Apply a thin coat of petroleum jelly to the top of another leaf.

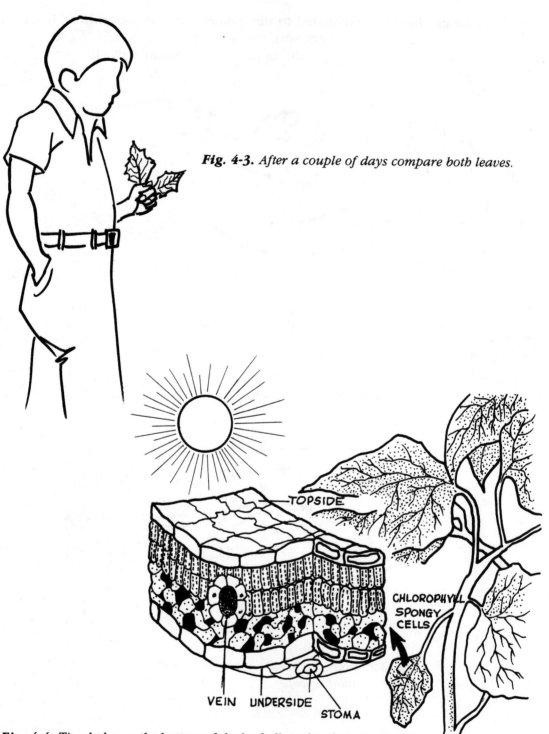

Fig. 4-3. *After a couple of days compare both leaves.*

TOPSIDE

CHLOROPHYLL
SPONGY
CELLS

VEIN   UNDERSIDE

STOMA

Fig. 4-4. *Tiny holes on the bottom of the leaf allow the plant to breathe.*

5

Why Plants Need Sunlight

Materials

- 2 BEAN PLANTS ABOUT THE SAME SIZE IN SEPARATE POTS

Place one of the plants in normal sunlight (Fig. 5-1) and the other in a closet or someplace where no sunlight can get to it (Fig. 5-2). Water each plant as you normally would to keep them growing. Then, after a couple of weeks, remove the plant from the closet and place it next to the one in normal sunlight.

Notice the difference in their color (Fig. 5-3). The one from the closet should have lost most of its green color. This is because it did not receive any sunlight. The plant needs sunlight for the production of food by *photosynthesis*. The energy from sunlight is changed into food.

Some plants, such as mushrooms, have no chlorophyll and grow in dark places (Fig. 5-4). They do not make food like green leaf plants. They use food that has been produced by green leaf plants.

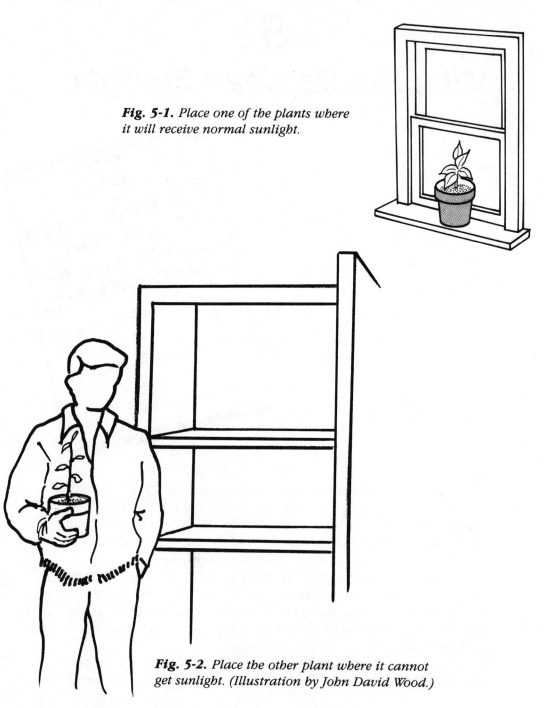

Fig. 5-1. *Place one of the plants where it will receive normal sunlight.*

Fig. 5-2. *Place the other plant where it cannot get sunlight. (Illustration by John David Wood.)*

Fig. 5-3. *Compare the color of the two plants.*

Fig. 5-4. *Mushrooms grow in dark places.*

6

How Plants Respond to Light

Materials

• SMALL POTTED PLANT (GERANIUM LILY ETC.,)

Place the plant in a sunny window and notice the position of the leaves (Fig. 6-1). Keep the plant there for several days and watch the way the leaves grow (Fig. 6-2). Now turn the plant around so that the other side faces the window (Fig. 6-3). A few days later, notice the change in the position of the leaves.

Plants respond to activity around them. The leaves of some plants fold together and droop when the plant is touched or shaken. The leaves of tulips close at night and open in the morning, and sunflowers turn toward the sun. The roots of plants respond to gravity by growing down. The stems and leaves of plants respond to the light by growing upward.

Fig. 6-1. *Place the plant in a sunny place.*

Fig. 6-2. *Notice that the leaves grow toward the sun.*

Fig. 6-3. *Turn the plant around and the other side will grow toward the sun.*

7

How Leaves Give Off Moisture

National E.

1962

Materials

- A THICK LEAF WITH A LONG STEM
- 2 GLASSES
- PIECE OF THIN CARDBOARD
- MODELING CLAY
- WATER
- PENCIL

Make a small hole in the center of the cardboard with the point of the pencil (Fig. 7-1). Push the leaf stem through the hole until the leaf almost rests on the cardboard (Fig. 7-2). The stem should continue several inches below the cardboard. Now press small pieces of clay against the cardboard and around the stem to seal the hole. This will prevent moisture from coming through. Fill one of the glasses with water and place the card on top of the glass (Fig. 7-3). The cardboard, with the leaf on top, should completely cover the top of the glass, and the stem should be in the water. Now put the empty glass upside down over the cardboard and cover the leaf (Fig. 7-4). Place the glasses in normal sunlight for a few hours.

Small drops of moisture will begin to appear on the inside of the top glass (Fig. 7-5).

The leaf gives off water that it has drawn up through its stem. This process is called *transpiration*. It is similar to *perspiration*, the production of sweat, in animals. Plants give off water mostly through tiny openings (stomata) on the surface of the leaves. The amount of water they give off depends mostly on how much was soaked up by the roots of the plant.

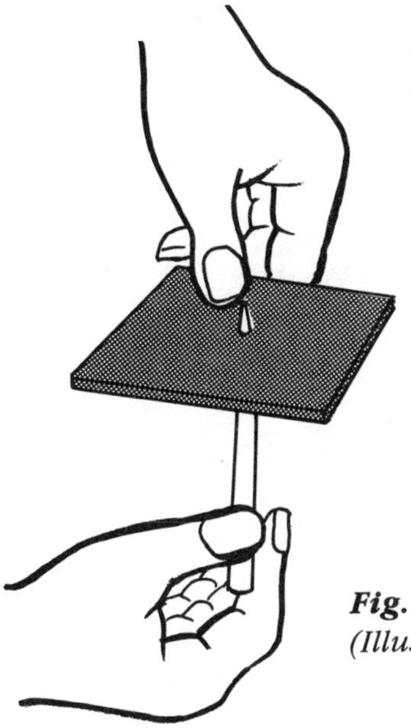

Fig. 7-1. *Make a small hole in the cardboard. (Illustration by John David Wood.)*

Fig. 7-2. *Push the stem through the hole in the cardboard.*

Fig. 7-3. Place the card on top of a glass of water.

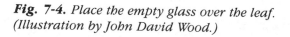

Fig. 7-4. Place the empty glass over the leaf. (Illustration by John David Wood.)

Fig. 7-5. *Moisture will form inside the empty glass.*

8
Why Leaves Fall

Materials

- BROAD TREE LEAVES (MAPLE, OAK OR ASH) IN AUTUMN AFTER THEY HAVE FALLEN

Look closely at one of the fallen leaves (Fig. 8-1). You will see that it has two main parts: the blade, and the stem, or *petiole* (Fig. 8-2). The blade is the broad part of the leaf that holds the green food-making cells. The stem holds the leaf to the plant, but it also brings water to the leaf and carries liquid food back from the leaf to all parts of the plant (Fig. 8-3).

During the summer, when the leaf is fully grown, it is producing large amounts of food. As summer continues, the young leaf begins to turn from a bright green to a darker blue-green.

Then something strange begins to happen in the base of the stem. A ring of cells, called *incision cells*, begins to turn into cork (Fig. 8-4). In late summer and early fall, these corky cells grow

23

across the stem and slowly block the tiny tubes that carry water and food to and from the blade. By early October, the water supply is completely cut off and the leaf stops making food. With its food supply cut off, the leaf loses its green color and reveals its hidden colors of yellow, red, and orange or purple. The leaf continues to hang on until the stem breaks off cleanly through the incision (cork) cells and flutters to the ground (Fig. 8-5).

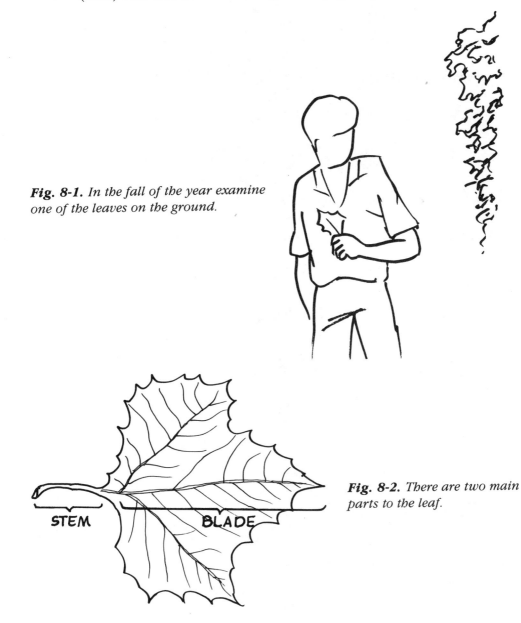

Fig. 8-1. *In the fall of the year examine one of the leaves on the ground.*

STEM   BLADE

Fig. 8-2. *There are two main parts to the leaf.*

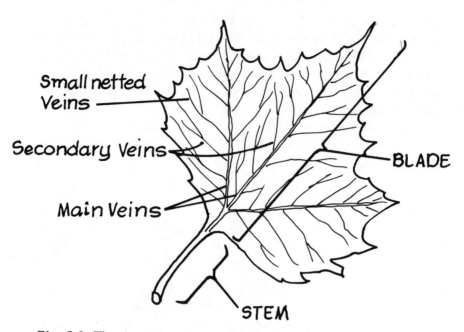

Small netted Veins

Secondary Veins

Main Veins

BLADE

STEM

Fig. 8-3. *The stem takes water to the leaf and carries food back.*

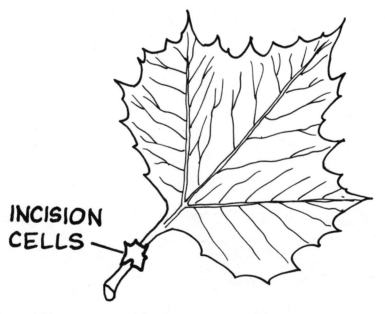

INCISION CELLS

Fig. 8-4. *In late summer incision cells turn into cork.*

Fig. 8-5. *The stem breaks clearly through the incision cells and the leaf falls to the ground.*

9
How to Preserve Leaves

Materials

- FULL-GROWN LEAF
- NEWS PAPERS
- HEAVY BOOKS (FOR WEIGHT)
- THIN CARDBOARD SQUARE OR RECTANGLE
- GLUE
- SHELLAC

Place the leaf flat between several layers of newspaper (Fig. 9-1) and put books on top of the papers for weight (Fig. 9-2). After one day, some moisture (wetness) from the leaf will be absorbed by the papers. Replace the wet papers with dry ones. After about three days, the leaf should be dried and pressed. Now glue the leaf to the cardboard (Fig. 9-3) and apply shellac to the entire surface (Fig. 9-4). When the shellac dries, your leaf will be preserved for your collection.

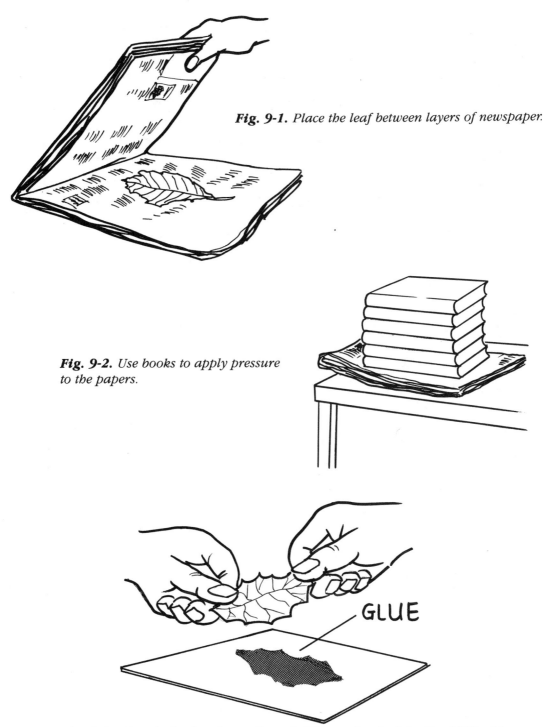

Fig. 9-1. *Place the leaf between layers of newspaper.*

Fig. 9-2. *Use books to apply pressure to the papers.*

GLUE

Fig. 9-3. *Glue the leaf to the cardboard. (Illustration by John David Wood.)*

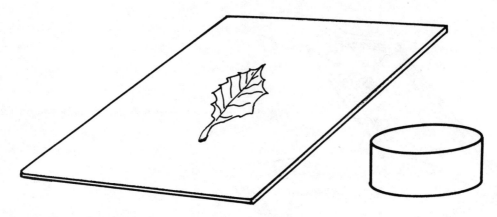

Fig. 9-4. *Apply shellac to the surface and your leaf will be preserved.*

10

Looking at the Age of a Tree

Materials

• THE TRUNK OF A TREE THAT HAS BEEN CUT DOWN

Look closely at the rings in the trunk (Fig. 10-1). These rings will tell you the tree's life story. Begin from the center and count a light and dark band as one year (Fig. 10-2). The center ring is the tree's first year of growth. The dark ring shows the growth in summer and the light band shows the growth in spring.

As you count outward from the center, the rings might be close together, showing that the tree grew slower because it was probably shaded from sunlight by other trees (Fig. 10-3). If the surrounding trees were cut down, the bands would be wider, showing that the growth speeded up. As a tree begins to reach its full size, the growth slows again and the bands become narrower.

Weather also affects the growth. During dry years the bands will be narrow, showing that the tree grew slower.

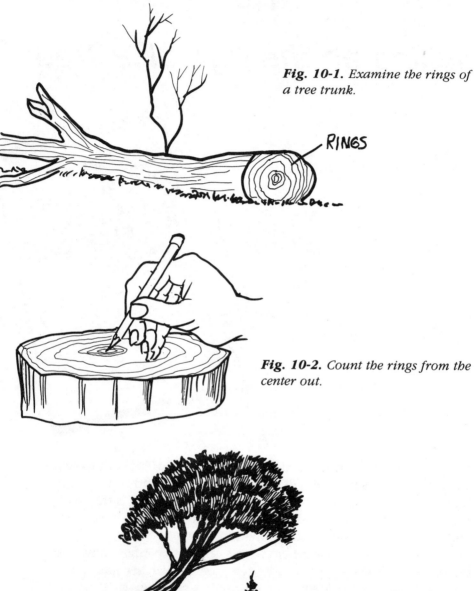

Fig. 10-1. *Examine the rings of a tree trunk.*

RINGS

Fig. 10-2. *Count the rings from the center out.*

Fig. 10-3. *Trees grow slower when they're shaded by larger trees.*

11
How Some Plants Produce New Shoots

Select a fairly long runner of an ivy plant. Beware of poison ivy! Bend the runner down to the ground (Fig. 11-1). Cover this section of the runner with damp soil (Fig. 11-2) and eventually it will root and grow a new plant. After the new roots have developed, the new plant can be cut from the parent stem. This method of producing new plants is called *layering*. Many plants reproduce this way naturally.

Fig. 11-1. *Bend a long ivy runner to the ground. (Illustration by John David Wood.)*

Fig. 11-2. *Cover a section of the runner with damp soil.*

12
How to Grow a New Plant from a Leaf

Materials
- AFRICAN VIOLET PLANT
- POT WITH POTTING SOIL
- LIQUID PLANT FOOD
- PLASTIC BAG

Break a leaf, with its stem, from the parent plant (Fig. 12-1) and plant it in the pot with about half of the stem covered by soil (Fig. 12-2). Keep the plant at room temperature. Water with liquid plant food every 14 days. High humidity (wetness in the air) is important. A plastic bag can be placed over the leaf to hold in moisture (Fig. 12-3). In a month, the leaf will have grown roots. In another 8 to 14 days, a new plant will appear, and in about 8 months, you should have a new adult plant.

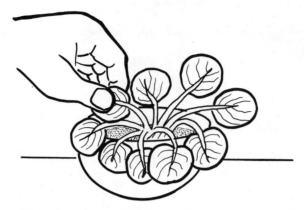

Fig. 12-1. Break a leaf and stem from the parent plant.
(Illustration by John David Wood.)

Fig. 12-2. Plant the leaf with about half
of the stem in the soil.

Fig. 12-3. A plastic bag will help
hold in the moisture.

13
A Look at Seeds

Materials
- A FEW MEDIUM OR LARGE DRIED BEANS OR PEAS
- MAGNIFYING GLASS
- BOWL
- WATER

Put the seeds in the bowl (Fig. 13-1) and cover them with water. Let them soak overnight. The next day, examine them closely and find a place on the seed where you can spread them open with your thumbnails (Fig. 13-2). After you have separated the seed, look at the inside of each of the two halves.

Notice the outer covering of the seed. This is the seed coat (Fig. 13-3). Inside the seed coat is a large area known as the "seed leaves," or *cotyledons* (Fig. 13-4). This is the food supply for the young plant that will grow from the seed. Now use the magnifying glass and look for the young plant. You should find a tiny pair of leaves (Fig. 13-5). You also might see the part that will become the root and stem of the future plant (Fig. 13-6). All plants, even the mighty tree, have such a small beginning.

Fig. 13-1. *Place a few bean seeds in a bowl and cover them with water.*

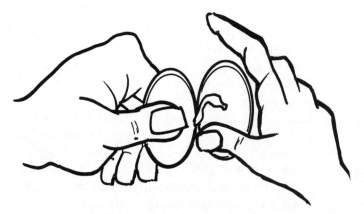

Fig. 13-2. *Use your thumbs to separate the seeds.*

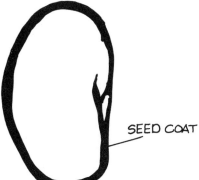

SEED COAT

Fig. 13-3. *The outer covering is the seed coat.*

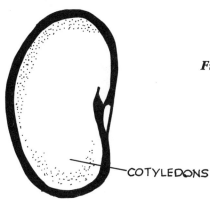

COTYLEDONS

Fig. 13-4. *The food supply is called the cotyledons.*

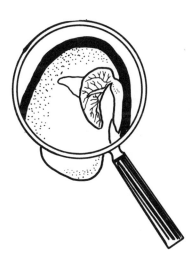

Fig. 13-5. *The tiny leaves of the young plant.*

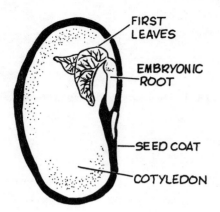

FIRST
LEAVES

EMBRYONIC
ROOT

SEED COAT

COTYLEDON

Fig. 13-6. Inside view of bean seed.

14

How a Bean Grows

Materials

- BEAN SEED
- SMALL JAR OR GLASS
- 2 PAPER TOWELS
- WATER

Fold the first paper towel into a strip about 4 inches wide (Fig. 14-1) and line the inside of the glass with it. Wad the other paper towel into a ball and place it in the circle formed by the first paper towel (Fig. 14-2). Now place the bean between the side of the glass and the paper towels, about an inch from the bottom of the glass (Fig. 14-3). You should have a clear side view of the bean. Next, pour water into the glass until the paper towels are completely wet (Fig. 14-4). Set the glass in a warm sunny place and you will see how a bean grows.

A few days after a seed has been planted, the young stem breaks out of the seed and begins to grow downward. It will form the main root and then the smaller roots (Fig. 14-5). While this is happening, the upper part of the stem quickly grows upward toward the sunlight, taking the seed and the food supply (the cotyledons) with it. Then the plant breaks through to the surface (Fig. 14-6). Now the cotyledons form the first leaves to appear above the surface (Fig. 14-7). They will store the food for the new plant (Fig. 14-8). The real leaves of the plant will grow from the tiny plant inside (Fig. 14-9). Within a couple of months, the plant will be producing bean seeds of its own.

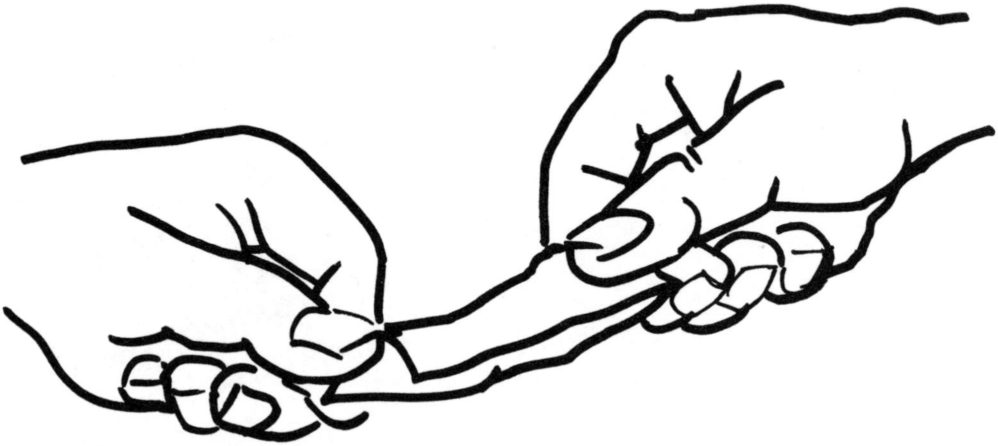

Fig. 14-1. *Fold the first paper towel into a strip and place it around the inside of the glass.*

Fig. 14-2. *Fill the opening with the other paper towel.*

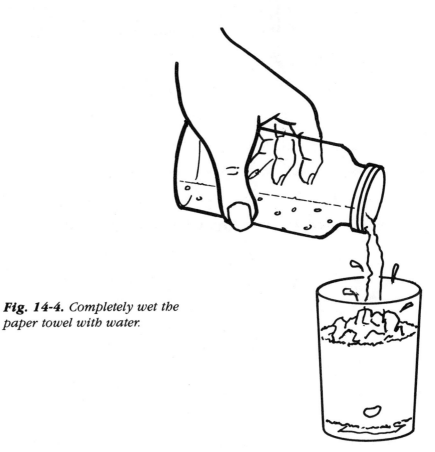

Fig. 14-3. Place the bean between the paper towels and the glass.

Fig. 14-4. Completely wet the paper towel with water.

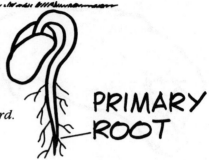

Fig. 14-5. *The primary root begins to grow downward.*

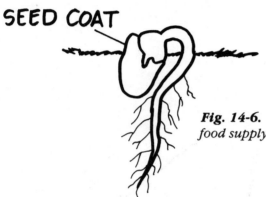

Fig. 14-6. *The plant breaks through the surface, taking its food supply with it.*

Fig. 14-7. *The cotyledons form the first leaves that appear above the ground.*

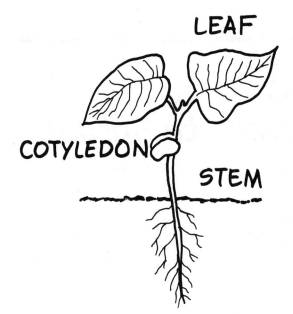

LEAF

COTYLEDON

STEM

Fig. 14-8. *The cotyledons store the food for the new plant.*

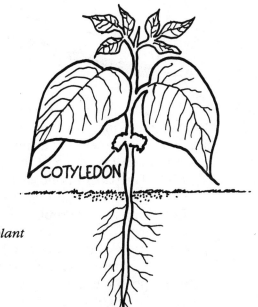

COTYLEDON

Fig. 14-9. *The real leaves of the new plant begin to develop.*

15
What a Seed Needs to Sprout

Materials

- 4 JARS
- 4 RUBBER BANDS
- PLASTIC FOOD WRAP
- 8 BEAN SEEDS
- 2 PAPER TOWELS
- WATER

Tear each paper towel in half so that you have four pieces. Fold each piece into a square that will fit in the bottom of the jars (Fig. 15-1). Place them flat against the bottom in each jar. Now pour a little water into three of the jars to completely wet the paper (Fig. 15-2). The paper in one jar should be kept dry. Place two beans on the paper in each jar (Fig. 15-3). Cover each jar with clear plastic food wrap and use rubber bands to hold it in place (Fig. 15-4).

Next, place the jar with dry paper and one with wet paper in a warm, sunny place. Put one jar with wet paper in the refrigerator, and the other jar with wet paper in a dark closet. You might want to number the jars and record the results. Number 1 could be labeled, "light and water." Number 2, "light and no water."

Number 3, "cold and water." Number 4, "no light with water" (Fig. 15-5). Notice the changes in the beans over the next several days.

Of the two jars in the sunny place, the seeds with water will be growing normally, and the ones without water will look just as they did when you put them in the jar. The seeds kept in the cold will be wrinkled but otherwise unchanged. The seeds kept in the dark, but with water, will have grown like the ones in the sun, except they will be completely white and have no color. These results tell you that plants need moisture, warmth and sunlight to develop.

Fig. 15-1. Fold the pieces of paper towels into small squares.

Fig. 15-2. Wet the paper towels in three of the jars with water.

Fig. 15-3. *Place two beans in each of the jars.*

Fig. 15-4. *Cover each jar with plastic food wrap.*

Fig. 15-5. *Label each jar.*

16
How to Grow a Hanging Garden

Materials

- A FEW ROOT VEGETABLES (CARROTS, TURNIPS, RUTABAGAS, ETC.)
- TOOTHPICKS
- STRING
- CURTAIN ROD IN A SUNNY WINDOW
- KNIFE

Cut about 1/3 off of the top of the vegetable (Fig. 16-1) and turn the top so that the cut end is up. Carve or scoop out the center area to form a small bowl (Fig. 16-2). Next, insert three toothpicks, evenly spaced, in the side of the vegetable (Fig. 16-3). Attach strings to the toothpicks and hang the vegetable from the curtain rod in a sunny window (Fig. 16-4). Now fill the hollow part of the vegetable with water, and your vegetable will grow (Fig. 16-5). Keep the hole full of water and turn the plant now and then so that the leaves will grow evenly (Fig. 16-6).

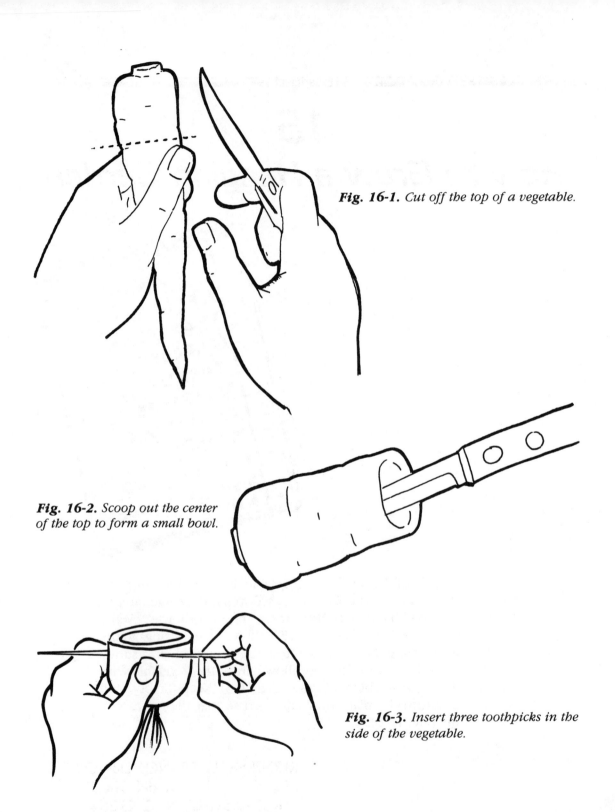

Fig. 16-1. *Cut off the top of a vegetable.*

Fig. 16-2. *Scoop out the center of the top to form a small bowl.*

Fig. 16-3. *Insert three toothpicks in the side of the vegetable.*

Fig. 16-4. Attach strings to the toothpicks.

Fig. 16-5. Fill the small bowl with water.

Fig. 16-6. Turn the plants around so the leaves will grow evenly.

17

How to Grow a Carrot Plant

Materials

CARROT
SAUCER
DRINKING GLASS
KNIFE
WATER

Cut off about one inch from the top of the carrot (Fig. 17-1) and place the cut end of the carrot top down in a saucer of water (Fig. 17-2). Cover the piece of carrot with the glass (Fig. 17-3). When the leaves begin to grow, remove the glass (Fig. 17-4).

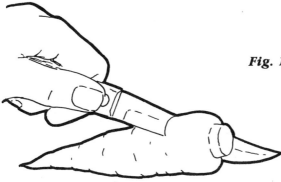

Fig. 17-1. *Cut off the top of a carrot.*

Fig. 17-2. *Place the top of the carrot in a saucer of water.*

Fig. 17-3. *Cover the carrot to keep in moisture.*

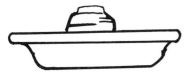

Fig. 17-4. Remove the glass when the leaves begin to grow.

18
How to Grow a Citrus Plant

Materials

ORANGE SEEDS
BOWL
SHALLOW PAN
SOIL
WATER
PLASTIC FOOD
WRAP

Pour water into the bowl and soak the seeds in the water overnight (Fig. 18-1). Fill the pan with about 1½ inches of soil (Fig. 18-2). Plant the seeds about ¼ inch deep and about 1 inch apart (Fig. 18-3). Moisten the soil with water (Fig. 18-4) and cover the pan with plastic (Fig. 18-5) to keep in the moisture. Now place the bag in a warm, sunny place. In about a week, you should see tiny sprouts. After they have grown to about 1 inch, you can move them to larger, individual pots.

Fig. 18-1. *Soak the seeds in water overnight.*

Fig. 18-2. *Fill a pan with soil.*

Fig. 18-3. *Plant the seeds about 1 inch apart.*

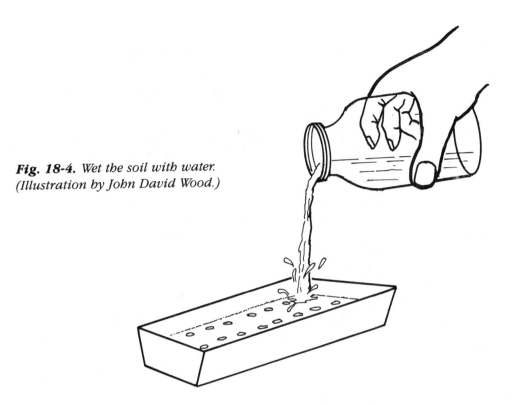

Fig. 18-4. *Wet the soil with water.*
(Illustration by John David Wood.)

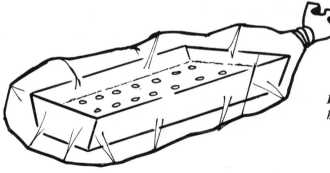

Fig. 18-5. *A plastic bag will hold in the moisture.*

19

Why a Compost Pile Gets Hot

Materials

FRESH LAWN
CUTTINGS
THERMOMETER

Make a packed layer of fresh lawn cuttings about 1 foot thick (Fig. 19-1). Place the thermometer inside for a few minutes and record the temperature (Fig. 19-2). Continue to take daily readings for the next several days (Fig. 19-3). You will see a steady rise in the temperature (Fig. 19-4).

Bacteria and fungi cause the partial rotting and decay of the grass. This decay produces heat as the rotting continues. A normal compost pile heats to between 120 and 160 degrees Fahrenheit by bacterial action. They can even catch fire. This is why damp hay can ignite and burn down a barn.

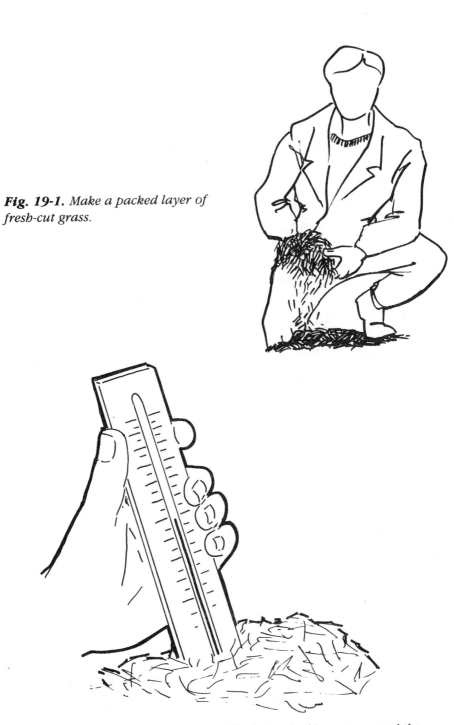

Fig. 19-1. *Make a packed layer of fresh-cut grass.*

Fig. 19-2. *Place the thermometer inside the packed grass to record the temperature.*

Fig. 19-3. Record the temperature for the next several days.

Fig. 19-4. You will see the temperature of the packed grass begin to rise.

20

How to Make a Compost Pile

Materials
- FALLEN AUTUMN LEAVES
- LAWN CLIPPINGS
- DEAD ANNUAL PLANTS, SUCH AS SQUASH VINES REMOVED FROM THE GARDEN
- HEAVY WIRE FENCING ABOUT

Materials
- 3 FEET HIGH
- WATER
- STICK

Find an out-of-the-way corner of the yard or garden and make a 4 to 5 foot diameter circle of the wire fencing (Fig. 20-1). Begin filling the area inside the fence with leaves and other clippings as they become available (Fig. 20-2). Tramp them down, and when you have a layer about 6 inches deep, water the layer well. Repeat the process for additional layers. It is important to keep the compost moist but not soggy (Fig. 20-3). Too much water and the pile loses oxygen, too little water and breakdown of the plant matter will stop. Use a stick to poke a few holes down into the pile to allow air to enter.

The bottom of the pile will become composted first. This means that you will need to turn the compost about once a year for fast, even composting. The process will take from 1 to 2 years, depending on the climate and the material in the pile. The high temperatures in the pile will kill most weed seeds and plant or animal disease organisms that might be present.

The contents of the pile will be turned into a crumbly product that contains many of the mineral elements needed for plant growth. When worked into the soil, it keeps the soil loose for easier growth of plant roots. It also allows water and air to get to the roots faster. The soil's water-holding ability is increased, too.

Fig. 20-1. *Make a circle of wire fencing.*

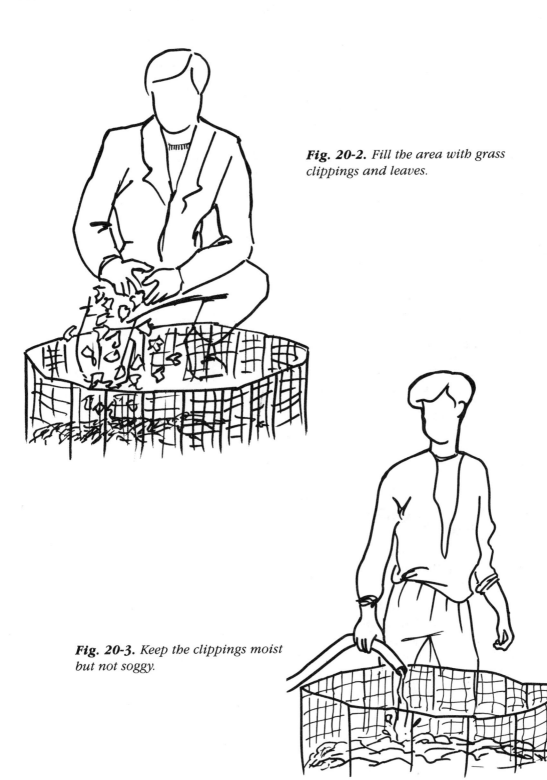

Fig. 20-2. Fill the area with grass clippings and leaves.

Fig. 20-3. Keep the clippings moist but not soggy.

21
Why Bread Molds

Place the bread outside for a few hours (Fig. 21-1), and then wet the bread and place it in the dish. Place the dish in a dark place (Fig. 21-2) and add a little water to the dish occasionally to keep the bread moist (Fig. 21-3).

After a few days examine the bread with the magnifying glass. You will see a fuzzy white growth (Fig. 21-4). This is a tiny plant that belongs to the fungi group, called *mold*. It is closely related to the mildews and mushrooms. Molds have no chlorophyll so they cannot make their own food. They must live on food made by other plants or decaying matter.

Common bread mold is a member of a group called black molds, because they produce dark-colored spores. Another group

Fig. 20-2. Fill the area with grass clippings and leaves.

Fig. 20-3. Keep the clippings moist but not soggy.

21

Why Bread Molds

Materials

- SMALL PIECE OF BREAD
- DISH
- WATER
- MAGNIFYING GLASS

Place the bread outside for a few hours (Fig. 21-1), and then wet the bread and place it in the dish. Place the dish in a dark place (Fig. 21-2) and add a little water to the dish occasionally to keep the bread moist (Fig. 21-3).

After a few days examine the bread with the magnifying glass. You will see a fuzzy white growth (Fig. 21-4). This is a tiny plant that belongs to the fungi group, called *mold*. It is closely related to the mildews and mushrooms. Molds have no chlorophyll so they cannot make their own food. They must live on food made by other plants or decaying matter.

Common bread mold is a member of a group called black molds, because they produce dark-colored spores. Another group of molds called blue molds also grow on bread. A green mold can often be found growing on various kinds of cheeses.

Molds develop from a tiny particle called the *spore*. The spores are carried by air currents. These spores settle on the bread and begin to swell and grow. They produce tiny threads that grow like roots while others spread out on the surface. As the plant body of the mold grows, it produces spore cases about the size of a pinhead that contain thousands of new spores (Fig. 21-5). Then these spore cases mature and break open. This allows the new spores to be carried away by air currents to settle on other damp foods and develop into new molds.

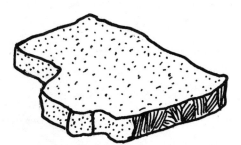

Fig. 21-1. Place the bread in the open air for several hours.

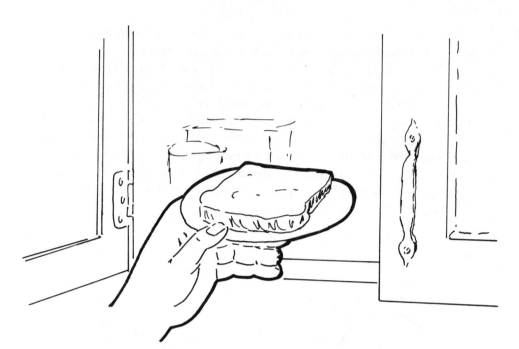

Fig. 21-2. *Place the bread in a dark place for a few days.*

Fig. 21-3. *Keep the bread moist.*

Fig. 21-4. *A fuzzy white growth will appear.*

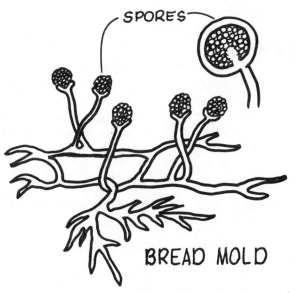

SPORES

BREAD MOLD

Fig. 21-5. *The plant body of the mold produces thousands of new spores.*

22

Spores from a Mushroom

Materials

- LARGE MUSHROOM OR TOADSTOOL
- PIECE OF PAPER

Break off the umbrella part of the mushroom (Fig. 22-1) and notice the gills on the underside. Place it on the piece of paper, with the gill side down, and leave it there several hours (Fig. 22-2). Then remove the piece of mushroom from the paper and examine the pattern left on the paper.

This is a spore print made up of thousands of spores (Fig. 22-3). A single spore is so small that it can only be seen through a microscope. Spores are carried on tiny stalks growing out from the surface of the gills and are responsible for growing new mushrooms (Fig. 22-4).

Fig. 22-1. *Break the top off the mushroom.*

Fig. 22-2. *Place it on a piece of paper for several hours.*

Fig. 22-3. *A spore print is made up of thousands of tiny spores.*

Fig. 22-4. *The tiny spores produce new mushrooms.*

23
Why a Puffball Smokes

Break open a puffball and you will see it give off tiny puffs of smoke. The smoke is really millions of spores (Fig. 23-1). This is how a puffball scatters its dusty spores into the wind. Puffballs are also called smoke balls and devil's snuffboxes. Some may grow to be more than 2 feet across. Puffballs are a type of mushroom that can grow in sunlight. They are fungi, like mushrooms. They cannot produce their own food, so they must grow in decaying matter.

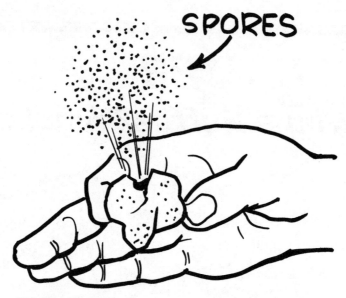

Fig. 23-1. *A puffball produces millions of tiny spores.*

24
The Cycles of a Fern

At certain times of the year the leaves, called *fronds*, of the fern develop brown patterns on their undersides. These patterns are made of hundreds of thousands of dusty particles called spores. When they appear, tap the leaf over the sheet of paper to collect the spores (Fig. 24-1). Then fill the pot with soil and peat moss with a layer of sand on top (Fig. 24-2). Now pour boiling water over the pot and its contents to destroy any bacteria that might attack the spores (Fig. 24-3). When the pot and its contents have cooled, sprinkle the spores on the sand (Fig. 24-4). Cover the pot with plastic food wrap (Fig. 24-5). Place the pot in a saucer of water to supply water from the bottom and let it stand for several weeks.

At this time you should see tiny green heart-shaped plants (Fig.

24-6). These plants are different from the original fern, and belong to a different generation. These are the plants that produce eggs and sperms. The sperms fertilize the eggs and then the eggs grow into mature fern plants. This process is called the *alternation of generations*. The large fern plant produces the spores, and the tiny fern plant produces the cells that grow into a large fern plant.

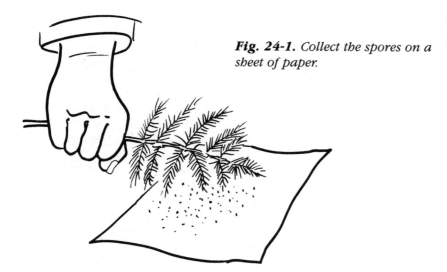

Fig. 24-1. *Collect the spores on a sheet of paper.*

Fig. 24-2. *Fill the pot with soil, peat moss and sand.*

SOIL

PEAT MOSS

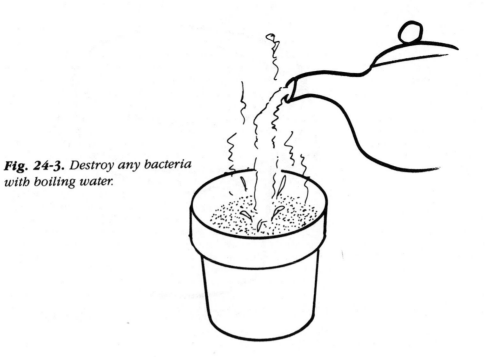

Fig. 24-3. Destroy any bacteria with boiling water.

Fig. 24-4. Sprinkle the spores on top of the sand.

Fig. 24-5. *Cover the pot with plastic to keep the moisture in.*

Fig. 24-6. *After several weeks tiny green plants will appear.*

25
Gas from a Banana

Materials
- BANANA (THAT STILL HAS A LITTLE GREEN ON THE TIP)
- 2 SMALL GREEN TOMATOES
- 2 JARS WITH LIDS

Put the banana in one jar and put a tomato in the jar with it (Fig. 25-1). Put the lid on to seal the jar. Now put the other tomato in the other jar by itself and screw on the lid (Fig. 25-2). Place both jars in a dark place at room temperature and see which tomato gets ripe first. You will see that the one with the banana ripens while the one by itself remains green (Fig. 25-3).

When fruit ripens, substances inside, called *enzymes*, bring about chemical changes. Enzymes break down the cells, soften the fruit and change the acid in the fruit to sugar. The green color fades as the chlorophyll collapses and the fruit gives off a gas called *ethylene*. A ripening banana is a good source of ethylene.

Farmers use this principle to prevent fruit from ripening too soon. They pick green fruit then gas it with ethylene so that it will be ripe at market time and not before.

Fig. 25-1. Put a banana and a tomato in one of the jars.

Fig. 25-2. Put a tomato in a jar by itself. (Illustration by John David Wood.)

Fig. 25-3. The tomato with the banana ripens first.

26
Red Dye from Beets

Materials

BEET
POT
WATER
STOVE

Boil the beet in a pot of water and the water will turn red (Fig. 26-1). This liquid can be used as natural dye. Early pioneers made dyes from various plants, roots and berries (Fig. 26-2). Red was made from the roots of a plant called madder and the bark from birch trees. Elderberries and the roots of the iris plant could produce a blue dye. Purple came from plums and dandelion roots. During colonial times in America, large plantations in the South grew indigo plants to produce a deep blue dye. Indigo is probably the oldest dye known. A garment discovered in Thebes, an ancient city in Greece, had been dyed with indigo about 3000 B.C. Today, however, dyes are produced in very large quantities in chemical plants.

Fig. 26-1. *Boiling a beet in water will produce a red dye.*

Fig. 26-2. *Early pioneers gathered berries to produce dyes.*

27

How to Grow an Avocado

Position the seed in the soil with the smaller, pointed end up and a little above the top of the soil (Fig. 27-1). Put the pot in a warm, sunny window (Fig. 27-2). Keep the soil moist and a tall tree-like plant will grow (Fig. 27-3). If you want a bushier plant, pinch off the growing tip when the plant is about 12 inches tall, and as branches appear and grow a few inches, pinch off the tips.

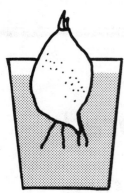

Fig. 27-1. Plant the avocado seed with the pointed end up.

Fig. 27-2. Place the plant in a warm sunny area.

Fig. 27-3. Avocado seeds produce tall treelike plants.

28
How to Grow a
Sweet Potato Vine

Materials

SWEET POTATO
GLASS OF WATER

Place the fatter part of the potato in a glass of water (Fig. 28-1) and put the glass on a window sill (Fig. 28-2). Soon roots will grow and then leaves. The vine can be kept growing in just water for many months, or you can plant it in a pot of soil to see how big it will grow (Fig. 28-3).

Fig. 28-1. *Put the sweet potato in a glass of water.*

Fig. 28-2. *Place the glass near a window.*

Fig. 28-3. *A sweet potato can grow into a large plant.*

29

How to Grow a Pineapple Plant

Materials

- TOP OF A PINEAPPLE
- PLANTING POT (ABOUT 6 OR 7 INCHES ACROSS)
- MOIST, SANDY POTTING SOIL
- KNIFE

Cut about 2 inches off the top of a pineapple (Fig. 29-1). Plant the top in a pot containing moist, sandy potting soil (Fig. 29-2). Continue to care for the plant. In about two years, the plant should be about 24 inches tall (Fig. 29-3).

Fig. 29-1. *Cut off the top of a pineapple.*

Fig. 29-2. *Plant the top in moist, sandy potting soil.*

Fig. 29-3. *The plant should grow about twelve inches a year.*

30
How to Sprout a Potato

Materials
- SMALL POTATO
- KNIFE
- LARGE BOWL
- DAMP SAND
- PLASTIC FOOD WRAP
- POTS WITH POTTING SOIL

Fill the bowl about half full of damp sand. Now cut the potato in half (Fig. 30-1) and plant each half, with the cut side down, in the sand (Fig. 30-2). Cover the bowl with plastic food wrap (Fig. 30-3) and put it in a dark place. Soon, you will see sprouts growing from the eyes of the potatoes (Fig. 30-4). Remove the cover and put the bowl in a sunny place. After they have grown a little more, you can move the plants to pots with potting soil.

The potato plant grows underground stems and roots. The tips of the stems, called *tubers*, grow into large food storage centers. This is the potato, the part we eat (Fig. 30-5). The "eyes" of the potato are the little dented spots. These are the stem and leaf buds.

Each section of potato with an eye contains enough stored food to keep the bud growing until the green leaves are large enough to take over the food production.

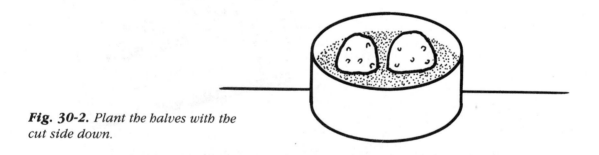

Fig. 30-1. *Cut the potato in half.*

Fig. 30-2. *Plant the halves with the cut side down.*

Fig. 30-3. *A plastic bag will keep the moisture in.*

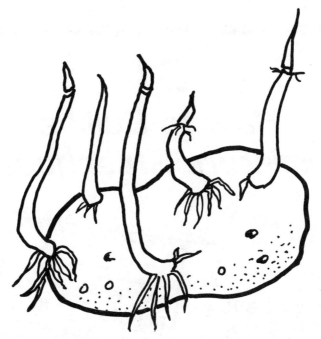

Fig. 30-4. *Sprouts will grow from the eyes of the potato.*

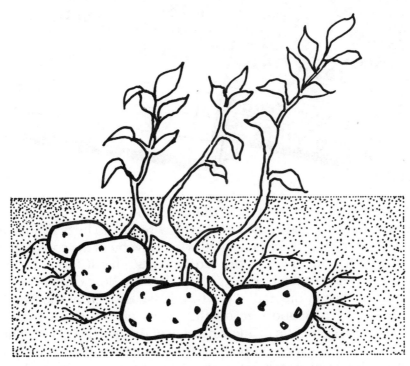

Fig. 30-5. *The tips of the stems produce the potato.*

31
How to Build a
Miniature Greenhouse

Materials

- SHALLOW CARDBOARD BOX
- WIRE CLOTHES HANGER
- CLEAR PLASTIC BAG (GARMENT BAG FROM DRY CLEANERS)
- WIRE TIE (FROM BREAD WRAPPER

Materials

OR TRASH BAG)
- PLIERS (TO BEND COAT HANGER)
- WIRE CUTTER (TO CUT COAT HANGER)

Cut the twisted part from the coat hanger and bend the wire into a square-shaped, upside down "U." The wire should be bent so that it fits over the top of the box lengthwise. Now press the ends of the wire into the top edges of the cardboard, so that it forms a loop over the center of the box (Fig. 31-1). Slide the box, endwise, into the plastic bag to the end (Fig. 31-2). Leave enough of the bag to close the opening and trim off the excess plastic. Cut a section from the excess plastic to line the inside of the box (Fig. 31-3). This will keep the moisture in the soil from damaging the cardboard. Fill the box with moist soil (Fig. 31-4) and plant your seeds or cuttings. Twist the opening together and tie it with the wire tie (Fig. 31-5). A greenhouse will allow you to control the climate and to start seeds or grow plants that otherwise would die in the open air.

Fig. 31-1. *Press the wire loop into the box.*

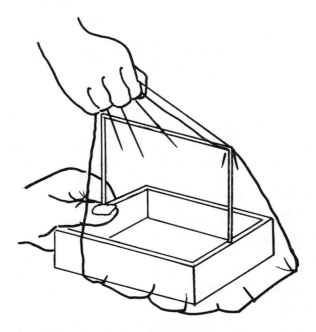

Fig. 31-2. *Slide the box into the plastic bag. (Illustration by John David Wood.)*

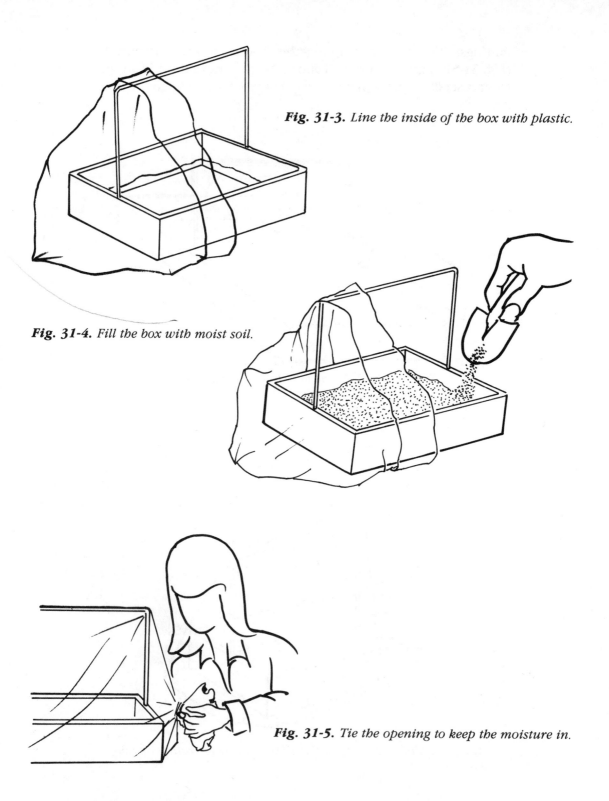

Fig. 31-3. Line the inside of the box with plastic.

Fig. 31-4. Fill the box with moist soil.

Fig. 31-5. Tie the opening to keep the moisture in.

32
How to Start Tiny Seeds

Materials

- TINY SEEDS PLANTED IN SMALL POTS OR BOXES
- CLEAR DRINKING GLASSES
- PLASTIC BAGS

Turn the glasses upside down over the planted seeds (Fig. 32-1). Place the seeds and glasses in a sunny area, but don't let the hot sun shine directly on the glasses. You can also place the pots or boxes inside plastic bags (Fig. 32-2). This keeps the moisture in until the seeds have a good start. When the sprouts are 1 inch high, you should remove the plastic bag in stages. First, take the bag off for an hour or two. Then leave the bag off for a half day at a time. Finally leave the bag off altogether.

Fig. 32-1. *Turn the glass upside down over the seed.*

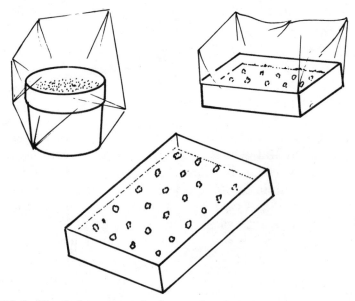

Fig. 32-2. *Plastic bags can also be used to help hold the moisture in.*

33
How to Take Root Cuttings

Materials
- LEAFY PLANT (SUCH AS A GERANIUM)
- SHARP KNIFE
- GLASS
- WATER
- MOIST SOIL

Use a sharp knife to remove about 6 inches of the top of the plant (Fig. 33-1). Next, strip away the lower leaves and place the bare stem in a glass containing about 2 inches of water (Fig. 33-2). The cutting also should root if it is inserted in moist soil.

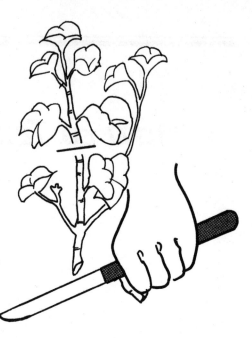

Fig. 33-1. *Cut about 6 inches off the tip of the plant.*

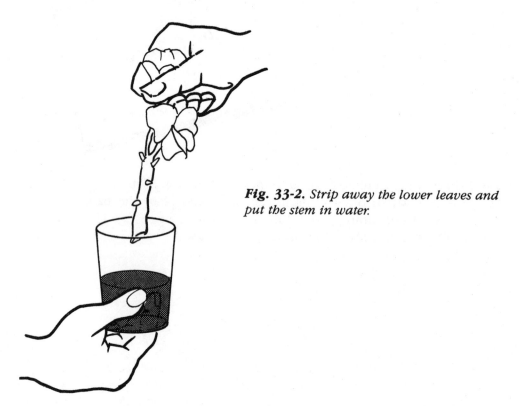

Fig. 33-2. *Strip away the lower leaves and put the stem in water.*

34
How to Pot a Plant

Materials
- PLANTING POT (6 INCHES TALL AND 6 INCHES ACROSS)
- PLANT (GERANIUM 12 INCHES TALL)
- SMALL PEBBLES
- SOIL

Place about a 1 inch layer of small pebbles in the bottom of the pot for drainage material (Fig. 34-1). Next, pour a mound of soil about 1½ inches high on top of the pebbles (Fig. 34-2). Now center the plant on top of the mound of soil and fill the surrounding area with more soil (Fig. 34-3). Secure the plant in place by packing in more soil to within 1 inch of the rim of the pot (Fig. 34-4). Leave 1 inch on top for watering.

Always use a pot about half the height or width of the plant you want to grow. For example, use a 6 inch pot for a 12 inch geranium. An African violet that had an overall leaf span of about 8 inches would need a 4 inch pot. New clay pots should be soaked several hours before they are used to prevent the clay from robbing the new plant of moisture.

Fig. 34-1. *Place a layer of small pebbles in the pot.*

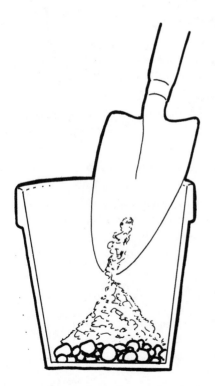

Fig. 34-2. *Pour soil on top of the pebbles.*

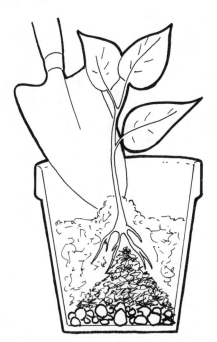

Fig. 34-3. Fill the area around the plant with more soil.

Fig. 34-4. Pack the soil to within 1 inch of the top of the pot. (Illustration by John David Wood.)

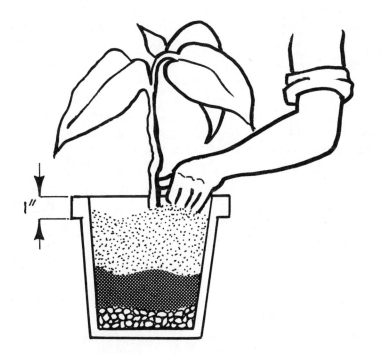

1"

35
How to Repot a Plant

Materials

- POTTED PLANT
- NEW POT (ABOUT 1 INCH LARGER ACROSS THE TOP THAN THE OLD POT)
- NEW SOIL

Place one hand across the top of the pot to catch the soil. Turn the plant upside down. Now gently tap the rim of the pot on the edge of a counter or table (Fig. 35-1). This should loosen the ball of soil and allow it to fall free (Fig. 35-2). Place the plant into the new pot (Fig. 35-3) and add new soil under and around it (Fig. 35-4).

Plants need repotting when they become ''rootbound'' or ''potbound.'' This is when the soil in the pot becomes matted full of roots.

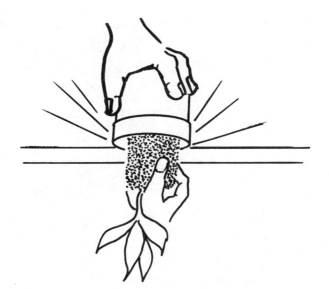

Fig. 35-1. *Gently tap the pot on the edge of a table. (Illustration by John David Wood.)*

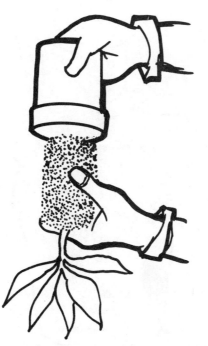

Fig. 35-2. *Catch the ball of soil as it falls free. (Illustration by John David Wood.)*

Fig. 35-3. *Place the plant into the larger pot.*

Fig. 35-4. *Fill the area around the plant with new soil.*

36
How to Graft a Plant

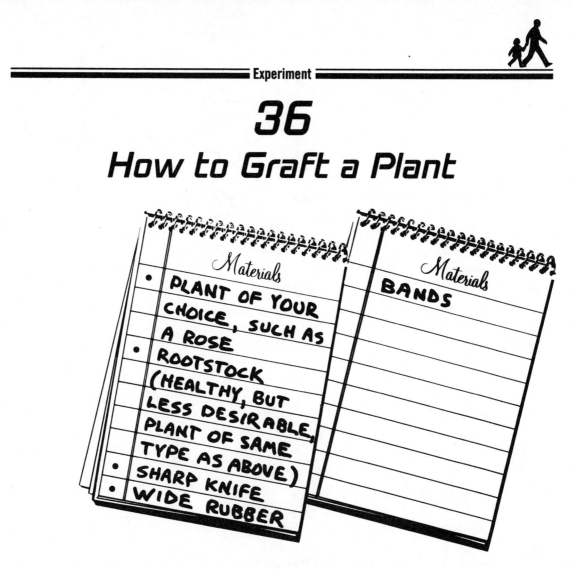

Materials
- PLANT OF YOUR CHOICE, SUCH AS A ROSE
- ROOTSTOCK (HEALTHY, BUT LESS DESIRABLE, PLANT OF SAME TYPE AS ABOVE)
- SHARP KNIFE
- WIDE RUBBER

Materials
BANDS

Carefully make a *T*-shaped cut through the bark of the rootstock plant. Now raise the flap of bark slightly to receive the bud graft from the other plant (Fig. 36-1). To remove the bud graft from the other plant, make a circular cut just below the base of the bud (Fig. 36-2). Cut off the leaves leaving about 1/2 inch of leafstalk (Fig. 36-3). Now slip the cut side of the graft into the T cut (Fig. 36-4) and tie into place with wide rubber bands (Fig. 36-5).

If the graft works, the bud graft will stay green. It will begin to swell in about a week, then grow leaves. After the new growth is well developed (next spring), the rootstock can be cut off to an inch or so above the graft (Fig. 36-6).

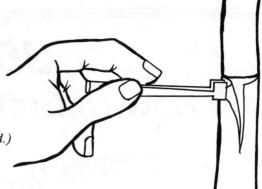

Fig. 36-1. *Make a T-shaped cut through the bark. (Illustration by John David Wood.)*

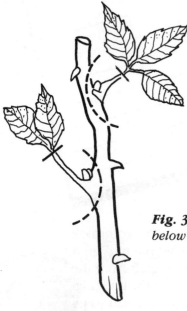

Fig. 36-2. *Make a circular cut below the base of the bud.*

Fig. 36-3. *Trim off the leaves of the bud graft.*

Fig. 36-4. *Place the cut side of the graft into the* T.

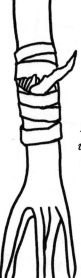

Fig. 36-5. *Fasten the cut together with wide rubber bands.*

Fig. 36-6. *After several months the unwanted plant can be cut away just above the graft.*

37

Root System of a Cactus

Materials
- SMALL CACTUS
- MAGNIFYING GLASS
- SHARP KNIFE
- PLANTING POT CONTAINING A MIXTURE OF SAND AND SOIL
- TONGS (TO HANDLE CACTUS)

Materials
- NEWSPAPER

Use the tongs (Fig. 37-1), or wrap the cactus with newspaper. The needles are sharp. Remove the cactus from its original container. Now examine the roots with the magnifying glass. You should be able to see the root hairs (Fig. 37-2). The plant takes in water through the root hairs.

Now cut off the root system (Fig. 37-3) and plant the cactus in the mixture of soil and sand (Fig. 37-4). Add a little water to the soil about once a week. After several weeks, take the cactus from the pot. Use the magnifying glass to examine the bottom of the cactus (Fig. 37-5). You should see a new root system developing. The cactus grows a long root system, spreading out in all directions. The roots lie close to the surface of the soil to quickly take in water.

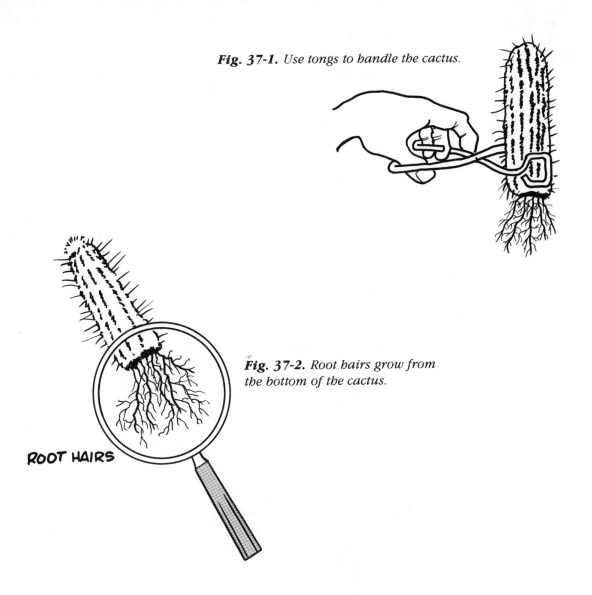

Fig. 37-1. *Use tongs to handle the cactus.*

Fig. 37-2. *Root hairs grow from the bottom of the cactus.*

ROOT HAIRS

Fig. 37-3. *Cut off the bottom of the cactus.*

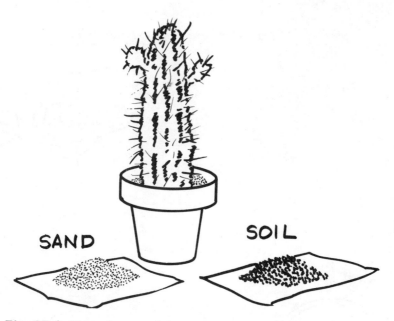

Fig. 37-4. *Plant the top of the cactus in a mixture of soil and sand.*

Fig. 37-5. *New root hairs will begin to grow.*

38
Cactus Plants and Water

Materials
- 3 SMALL CACTUS PLANTS (IN POTS)
- MEASURING CUP
- WATER
- PENCIL AND PAPER

Place the plants near each other so that they get equal amounts of sun (Fig. 38-1). Number the plants 1, 2, and 3 (Fig. 38-2). Now give plant 1, a small amount of water. Water plant 2 with about the same amount of water you would give a regular house plant. Then give plant 3 an excessive amount of water (Fig. 38-3). Continue to care for the plants and record their growth and the amount of water each plant receives. You should see that the extra measure of water is little help to a cactus plant.

Because rain seldom falls in the desert, plants must get by with very little water. Cactus plants survive these long, dry spells by storing water in their trunks.

Fig. 38-1. Place the plant so each one gets the same amount of sun.

Fig. 38-2. Label the plants.

Fig. 38-3. *Give extra water to the third plant.*

39

Flat-Grafting Cactus Plants

Materials

- 2 SMALL CACTUS PLANTS (IN POTS)
- SHARP KNIFE
- 4 RUBBER BANDS
- TONGS (TO HOLD PLANTS)

Cut off part of the top of each plant (Figs. 39-1 and 39-2) and trim the corners of the cut edges. Replace one top with the other, putting the cut sides together (Fig. 39-3). Now loop two rubber bands over the tops of each plant and around the bottom of the pot to hold the graft until the parts grow together (Fig. 39-4).

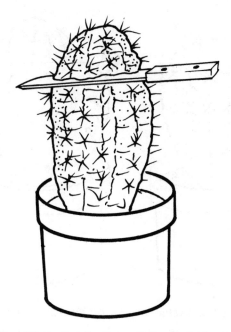

Fig. 39-1. *Cut the top off the first plant.*

Fig. 39-2. *Cut the top off the second plant.*

Fig. 39-3. *Exchange one top with the other.*

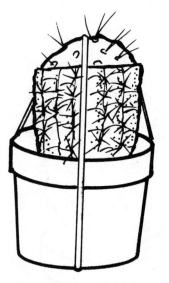

Fig. 39-4. *Use rubber bands to hold the cut edges together.*

Science Fair Projects

Science fairs are becoming more popular because they provide an exciting and different way of learning. They also offer the chance to share learning with family and friends. A successful science fair project requires a lot of planning. One of the most important parts of the planning is deciding on the subject. Don't pick a subject too quickly. Give it a lot of thought. Otherwise you might discover later that the material was either too expensive, or not available, or that the project was just too difficult. This could stop the project at a time when it would be too late to start another. Your project will be more enjoyable if you pick a subject you like, one you are familiar with or one you would like to know more about. Use your imagination, but keep your project within your abilities.

You might begin your planning by dividing your project into basic steps such as: (1) choosing a topic, (2) finding questions and a *hypothesis*—simply what you think the results of your experiment will be, (3) doing the experiment and (4) recording results and conclusions of your experiment.

A successful project requires research. This can include writing a research paper (Fig. 40-1). A research paper will be a big help in gathering information. It will also help you narrow your subject to a specific topic.

You may want to write a report on your experiment. This should explain what you wanted to prove or a question you wanted answered. You might use graphs and charts to explain your experiment (Fig. 40-2). Your report should describe your experiment, the results of your experiment, and the conclusions you made based on the results of your experiment.

When choosing an experiment, consider the materials you will need. It might be necessary for you to build a model. Models can usually be made from wood or cardboard. Don't overlook items that are usually thrown away (Fig. 40-3), items such as empty coffee cans, plastic or glass bottles, cardboard tubes from paper towels and empty wooden spools from sewing thread. Be creative. Use your imagination.

After you have selected the topic of your project, narrow it to a specific question to answer. Have a definite problem to solve or a point to prove. For example, if you wanted to prove that plants prevent erosion, you could show an example of how rains wash away bare soil. Then show a drawing of a plant's roots grasping the soil. This could lead to describing the importance of seeding range lands to save the soil.

You might want to prove that plants take in carbon dioxide and give off oxygen. You could show this with your experiment, and then show how important plants are to the air we breathe. This also could include the role areas like the rain forests play in the climate we have.

If you were interested in the subject of grafting, you could show how plants that do not grow well in one type of soil could be grafted on stock that does grow well in that particular soil. This might increase the food supply for people in countries that have poor soil.

If your experiment will be displayed on a table, you could place it on a wooden or cardboard panel (Fig. 40-4). The two ends can be angled forward so that the panel will stand by itself, something like a theater stage.

You can mount posters on the panel that contain information about your experiment (Fig. 40-4). The panel could include information from your research paper or report. The left section of the panel might show the purpose of your experiment, why you chose that project or what you wanted to prove. The center section of the panel could show a detail of your experiment: a root system, a graft, etc. The right section of the panel could show the results of your experiment. It could include the conclusions you made and possible uses for this information that might benefit people.

Plants have been around a long time, but we still have much to learn about them. Medicine is just one of the fields that would benefit from more information. Scientists can only guess at the important new medicines that are waiting to be discovered in plants growing wild in different parts of the world.

Fig. 40-1. *A research paper provides help in gathering information. (Illustration by John David Wood.).*

Fig. 40-2. *Use charts and grafts to help explain your experiment.*

Fig. 40-3. *Throwaway items can often be used in your experiment.*

Fig. 40-4. *Posters mounted on the panel will help explain your experiment.*

Glossary

bacteria Tiny plants that can be seen only with a microscope.

chlorophyll The green coloring matter in plants.

cotyledons The first leaves that sprout from a seed, manufacture food for the new plant.

enzymes A protein-like substance found in plants and animals that speeds up specific chemical reactions.

fungi Plural for fungus, a plantlike organism that does not contain chlorophyll and cannot make its own food.

generation Any of the stages of successive improvement in a plant, system, etc.

graft A plant consisting of a rooted part into which another part has been inserted so that both parts will join (grow) together.

hypothesis A guess used by scientists to explain how or why something happens.

layering To grow a plant by bending down and partly covering a living plant with earth so that it may take root.

organism A living animal or plant.

petiole The stalk of a leaf.

photosynthesis A food-making process where green plants combine energy from light with water and carbon dioxide to make food.

spore A single cell that can grow into a new plant.

stoma A microscopic opening in the leaves of plants, surrounded by guard cells, that allow the plant to breathe.

transpiration The loss of water vapor from a plant.

tubers A swollen underground stem.

Index

581.078
WOO   Wood, Robert W.

        Science for kids